Beautiful People and Words

A Collection of Poems from Around the World

To Family and Friends

Book design by Rehna Mathews, Swekchha Luitel, Marin and Twila Richards.

Cover design by Rehna Mathews, Twila Richards, and Yuvika Tharayil.

ISBN: 978-1-7377460-0-3
Imprint: True House Publishing

Foreword

We are a group of beautiful poets who all met through social media. Rehna, the creator and the curator of the group, started the room with Aakash. The room was named *Become a Published Poet in 100 Days*. Ever since then, the room has been running with the same name as a reminder of its purpose. Soon, they were joined and supported by three inspiring women Twila, Amee, and Swekchha and started meeting over Zoom. Now, their group is thriving with more numbers of poets: Anmol, Natassha, Vincent, Deep, Nishanthan, and Mir. They are continuing to grow with more beautiful poets in the group. Later, these people became a family of global poets, coming from different parts of the world. The group started working on their first collaborative book named *Beautiful People and Words*. This is the book that includes the favourite poems of these poets from around the globe.

Beauty Found Through Diversity

These group of people are
The beauty found through diversity...
I met them in a room
A room full of love and respect
Slowly and gradually...
We started calling each other
Our second family
Yes, we are this wonderful group of people
Who are the beauty found through diversity.
We share poems with each other
But it really is love we exchange
We inspire creativity in each ither
But it really is a positive energy that we exchange
One day we all hope to meet in person
Bring the whole wide world in one place
We will share the love and respect in person
Crack jokes and laugh on how small the world is
Our roots are deepened and spread
Beyond the reach of just lands
We are whole and together
We are complete with each other
Yes, we are the kindest group of people
Who are the beauty found through diversity!

Swekchha

Aakash Khurana

Aakash Khurana is a young poet and an entrepreneur from Himachal Pradesh, India. Aakash considers his family and his words most important to him. If he isn't playing football or table tennis, you can almost always find him reading or writing. His writings are mostly about love and life. He always tries to add values to his life and to everyone around him through his poems.

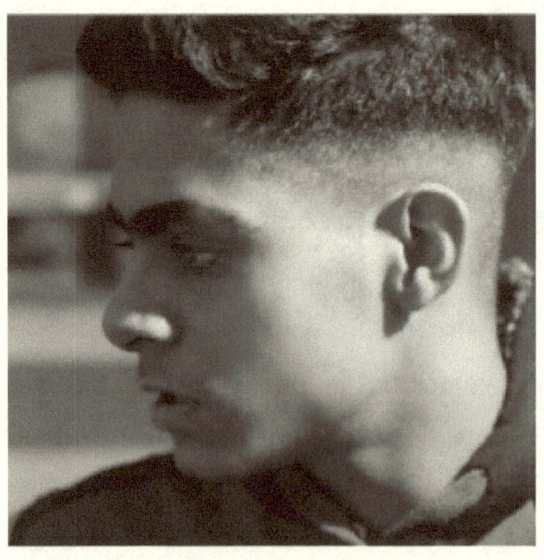

HoPe...

I quit!
I really quit. I can't live.
In this shit! My ideas are flop.
But I don't wanna stop!
Dreams I had too.
Can do better than you.
But I ain't such.That has much!
A hope still lives. In my heart.
Can I make a start ?
I think so.
But have nothing to show!
Well no one cares. And no one cared!
I do. I do love me!
Wanna be free.
Free isn't all that I desire.
I wanna be the fire!
That burns.
Please help me learn.
So that I can see. The beautiful me!
But this shit is not gone.
And I still have not won!
A hope still lives in my heart.
God make me smart. Make me blessed!
As I am messed!   Am I?
Okay I need some rest.
I am so confused. I feel used!
But this hope has never gone.
Because I was wrong. I can feel!
Let's make a deal!
I will prove. So I can remove.
All the negativity. That I was pity!
But wow! Everything's good now!
I started laughing. And grew tough!
Because that hope was enough..

TO HEAVEN...

Dad,
I feel sad.
Save me,
Or I'll become mad.
Things aren't good.
Like it should.
I'm not a kid.
But no one's telling me,
What I did.
This feel,
Can't be healed.
If possible then do it please.
Or give me the keys,
To heaven.
Yes I wanna die.
Let's give it a try.
Ohhh but I'm already dead.
No tears left to shed.
Now that you've come.
I dunno what I've become.
It's late.
Ohhh wait!
I think it's just started.
Or I think too much.
Maybe..
You said!
It's pretty sure,
That it can cure.
Your words felt pure.
Unlike me.
The poor me.
Walking,
With no one else talking.
The hope u gave,
While singing a song.
I dunno what's gone wrong.
Again,
I felt pain.
Yes in heaven too!
Nothing to say much.
I bid you adieu...

My LiFe'S a...

My life's a play.
Running all the way.
From here and there.
Heading towards nowhere.

My life's a lie.
I think.
I can't die.
But that day is not so far.
When it'll be all bizarre.

My life's a dream.
Just want an ice cream.
I can't have it, what?
Please, it's so hot.

My life's fun.
But it's so dark.
Without a Sun.

My life's a river.
But I can't float.
I shiver.
Without a boat.

My life's a little.
With a big mess.
And a heart much brittle.

My life's not a life.
Worth living.
All I am doing is giving.
Excuses!

My life's a path.
So unusual.
All those excuses.
I forget for a while.
What matters is that juvenile.
Whose one thing changed everything.
And that was his smile!

It's JUST...

It's just that I was hurt.
No one could see.
The crying me.
No one wanted to.
They have their own lives.
But I wanted to reach the skies.
It's just a dream wow.
What the hell now.
All those people,
Who saw me as a fool.
Wasn't that so cool?
Not for me though.
It's just a few words,
That made me sad.
Why were you all so bad?
Couldn't keep it in your own mind.
And be just a little kind.
Cause I don't have beard,
Was I too weird?
No I don't think it as a reason,
For which I was being convicted of treason.
Well there's none!
Because I was innocent.
And you knew it right.
It's just I was too bright.
That u couldn't bear this light.
So u thought,
To make it dark.
And bark.
So much that,
It felt deep.
I wasn't able to sleep.
It's just I was really a fool.
Instead I could have been cool.
Like a swimming pool.
But I was listening to you.
Forgot that I have my own mind.
That is so kind.
Forgot that I have my own life.
But now you cannot do anything,
Because I took it with my own knife!

LoVe IS UNconditional...

His sister's so kind,
Unlike him.
The boy with the mouth.
That only shouts!
This day she cried.
After so long.
Remembered the last time when her parents were gone.
But today because of his brother,
Whom she loves more than her mother.
She's feeling so bad.
Missing her dad.
Who called her dove.
But she lost that love.
She was fine until her brother hit her.
Today is unbelievable.
She ran away from the slum.
Didn't realise whether she'll be able to come,
Back again.
But she's feeling so much pain.
Her brother in search,
Reached the church.
Found some people hurrying,
And he started worrying.
Went closer.
And found her sister lying.
In front of the church road almost dying.
A tear came out.
He wanted to shout.
Found something strange.
Looked from a closer range.
Was a bouquet of flowers.
In her hand.
With a letter band.
Written 5 words on it were,
"Brother, I love you forever!"
At that moment he missed her more than ever.
He started screaming.
But realised he was dreaming!
When her hand on his face,
He suddenly jumped from his bed.
And hugged her tightly.
Looked at her eyes,
Asked her never to leave ever.
And atlast said these 5 words,
"Sister, I love you forever!"

FeeL IT CLOSE to YoU...

Show me,
Yeah! Show me what you have.
Man.
You can.
No? Ohh!
So?
It's okay I'll show.
The love!
Just look above.
Yeah!
Clouds in the sky.
That Happiness u can't buy.
Down!
Or the whole town.
Depends upon how you see.
Can you be like me?
Nope! Never!
Everyone's unique.
Speak!
Don't be weak.
You can have the power.
Just look at that flower.
It's lovely too!
And so do you.
Those mountains.
Or let it be fountains.
The pleasure is everywhere.
But you have to care.
For this air!
Or die.
U can't even try!
The dead are gone.
They haven't won.
But you can win.
Nature is beautiful.
We all have to be dutiful.
For what!
Mother Earth has given.
This heaven!
Can't have it even in the dreams.
Please!
Save it!
Or
Die listening screams...

MY...

My feelings untold. My
heart sold. My

body ache. My
birth mistake. My

wound deep. My
eyes weep. My

talents amused. My
mind confused.

REALITY...

Are we living a great life?
Well it starts with the phone.
Watching the lives of the unknown.
Feeling jealous in the morning itself.
Indeed a great start!
With a broken heart.
Couldn't stop scrolling!
It's your life but someone else is controlling.
Want to be like that celebrity?
I bet you can't.
Isn't that pity?
Considering others' opinions.
Even when you believe in yourself.
Want to be rich, want to be happy.
Want to be fit and travel a lot.
But wondering u cannot.
Why? Those excuses are stopping you.
No one can stop you unless you allow it.
So get off your bed.
There's a beautiful life ahead!

Can You Guess It?

Atoms together make a cuboidal.
A thing with no wing.
But can fly much higher with it.
A beautiful front.
With a blurb on the back.
Lightweight and great.
A small one.
With a large amount of information.
Truly awesome for vacation...

Hey! Beautiful...

Hey!
You are my girl.
Light that you made bright.
Shines on me all night.
Star you are.
The only one in the sky.
Hope we both can fly.
Can see heaven.
Or the sisters' seven.
Life is beautiful just like you.
I have lost my mind.
Cannot find.
Anything,
Prettier than you!
Even the flowers look fade.
Look at you,
What God has made!
All those creatures.
And the moon.
Will kneel down.
Pretty soon!
But you will rise.
And will live the queen size.
To all those who haven't seen this beauty before or will tomorrow.
For them I feel so sorrow!

No ReGrEtS...

From the top of the mountains to the bottom of the sea.
I jump to find.
But cannot get what I want.
Then I rise.
But fell a thousand times.
I wish to rise again.
It's hard.
But that's life.
And I lived it.
Without regrets!

I miss.. I wish..

I miss..
I miss those days of happiness.

I miss those moments of pleasure.
I miss those people of wisdom.

I miss those acts of kindness.
I miss those words of appreciation.

I wish..
I wish I could relive those memories.

I wish at least in the dreams.
I wish I could sleep..

HAIKUS...

You are truly mine.
Cannot go away from me,
Happiness undefined.

Life is piano.
Sometimes its white, sometimes black.
But pretty as whole.

Smile always my dear.
It's the source of everything,
But it costs nothing.

Just close your eyes please.
Think of something beautiful,
it's totally you.

Amee Bee

Who, Amee? (Amee, is pronounced UH-ME, like yummy, except without the -Y) Amee means unconditional love in Sanskrit. Amee Bee is a magical artist, prolific poet and calming storyteller, born in America of Indian Gujarati descent. She is 100% inspired by love. Without professional lessons in art (or poetry), she began to paint one cold January Morning in 2017, and prolifically wrote 2,000 love poems by 2018 that year. She has lost count of thousands of poems since then. She aims to find love and beauty in what's around her, be appreciative of what she has-as well as being in love and playing with her nightly Love and Respect poetry family. It's her secret to happiness. Art, poetry and stories are what translate from it. By sharing, she hopes you too experience the love and magic within you.

Life isn't about

I cried yesterday
Only to smile today
To remember
Life isn't about what I
Receive
But how I can
Serve others
With love
And not expect
Anything in return

Love pieces me together

It's okay to be forgotten
For my beloved
Remembers me
And tugs on
Memory strings
Reminding me
I'm here
I'm human
just to
Come back home
For if I expect love
From
The ones I'd wish to
Get it from
And add the burden
Of how I'd like to receive it
On each one
My heart would break
For it has before
countless times
And now it's a mosaic
Sealed by love
Pieced together by
Strangers
Who have become
family

When they part

What if love wasn't
Destined for one person?
Yet it is to discover
That one soul
we share
For each night
Or each morning
We send kisses to the moon
Or wave to the sun
Sending messages
To the ones we love
That reside on the
Other side

Togetherness

In her tomorrow
While he shares his sorrows
While she listen's
in his yesterday
The Kashmiri birds chirp
To his words
to Keep them present
To experience
the beauty in their own world
For he speaks from his
Heart
And when one speaks from
the heart
there's togetherness
—No one is apart

Don't question it, just enjoy it.

Gather a group of lovers
And bring the sad
I guarantee
Night, after night
The sadness will slip from their
Heads
And in madness
They will smile and wonder
"What is this gladness?"

No matter

No matter your faith
No matter your belief
Our daily ritual
is proof
gathering in love
accepting
and supporting
each other as we are
Uplifts us from depression
Gives hope to
Humanity
And makes us resilient
Enough to offer
Compassion

Miracles

In a 100 days time
I have seen miracles in
Front of my eyes
I've seen the guarded
Loosen up and let love in
I've seen the sad ones
become glad ones
I've witnessed the power of
Listening is just as
Powerful as expressing
I've learned loving one another
Truly heals

Poetry Ice Cream Shop

Welcome to the poetry
Ice cream shop
We have flavors from
Around the world
Poets adding spicey words
inspired by their day
Some can make you feel
The color blue
By listening
The taster and the
expresser heals
While others will
Wash it away with magic
And transport you to
A whole new world
through their stories
You come out of it
Full from receiving
all the love they're
pouring

Love

Hi love!
 Hello Love
  Love you love
   Love to love, love
 Love love, love
Loooove!

What can I do?

If I can not
Speak you into
Existence
If I cannot demand
Your presence
If I cannot
Force your appearance
What can I do
To bring you here?
"Love me dear"
Is what I silently hear.

A poem inspired by a lightbulb
Swekchha Vincent and Amee

Light bulb

I light up
When
You turn me
On
It's as if I
Hit Nirvana
Nirvana has never
Seen a light
As bright that shines
Don't worry
You can't turn me off
I won't ever blow a
Fuse on you
I'm just a light
Showing a
Way

Anmol Shakya

Showing the trust of love across the globe from Nepal. Back in the day when life was like dark clouds in the sky, or when it was all rainbows, he lifted his pen to jot down words. His intuition let him to flow and fly through the bits and pieces of troubles he had. Through this he slowly became generous and kind to the world. His understanding "Peace denotes the yin and yang, life denotes the darkness and light through which all of us experience". He walks through this journey finding out the meaning of life. His name "Precious".

Gratitude

~ Precious ~

Gratitude,
For the life that's given
For the profound intelligence
For I and world to be connected

I, a human being
Being conscious of who I am
I acknowledge the power of Universe
From the small place I stand

I, a consciousness
I am aware of my surroundings
My body, just a material form
My soul, a divine energy

Angel from the Heaven

~ Precious ~

There's this girl, I see everyday
She lives across the street, not so far away
Maybe she is a princess from a lost kingdom
I think she is an angel, dropped from the heaven

Her eyes are pretty, shiny blue
Looks so stunning, I am out of clue
Her curly hair, it makes my heart go high
Those red lips, oh it makes me wanna fly

I wonder if she's a star, fallen from the sky
Wonder if she is that fairy, from the book of my life
This heart beats faster as I look to her
I freeze to death when she comes near

I have never seen a beauty, never such a thing
She makes my heart start to tingle and swing
She's precious than gold, she's precious than diamond
Her soul is so pure, as an angel from the heaven

Dream

~ Precious ~

I had a dream today
You and I were together
We were so happy then
Nothing in the world mattered

At a lovely place we were
Where no one else was found
Where birds chirped songs loud
With flowers and trees all around

It so felt my destiny, I be with you
Throughout all my life ahead
To love you with all my heart
As the time slowly goes by

How the feel you had given me
I cannot even explain
When I kissed your sweet lips slowly
The memories I cannot retain

The time was teasing me
As I looked you only a second
The day was ending on speed
The moment gone so quickly

I miss the dream I had today
As I woke up without you
Because we were so happy then
Nothing in the world mattered
Nothing in the world matters

What is happiness?

~ Precious ~

What is happiness?
For someone,
With an empty stomach
Working so hard all day
Sleeping in the streets
With no food or clean water
Begging, for a better life

For someone,
Discriminated
Hated for their existence
Treated as a burden
Treated badly by their own parents
Seen as a value of nothing
Lived their whole life in vain

For someone,
Who was abused
Were accused for their innocence
As they were raped, sold, molested
The unsaid stories
Torn apart with profound degree for pain

For someone,
Who lost a child
Infront of their eyes
As there was no money to cure
Because people are insecure
And they hate one another
Wars exist, people lost lives
Fight endlessly for no purpose
With an absence of humanity
Blood shed like river

What is happiness?
How did humanity get here?

Growing up

~ Precious ~

There was a time once upon
Upon a hill there was this kid
He woke up every day to dawn
The sunrise he never missed

There was this kid who had dreams
The light in him that sparked
Saw moon and stars every night
Smiled all days as he walked

Life has become a hard journey
As today times are tough
Love has begone far away
From everyone the heart had touched

Somewhere, along the long journey
Life's essence out of way
Only left is all the reminisces
He misses himself today

He missed the kid once upon
Who climbed the hill at dawn
Saw moon and stars every night
Walked with the light to shine on

Realizations

~ Precious ~

Like the river flows to make oceans
Life goes, on and on till the end comes
The ups and downs, many struggles and
obstacles
We tackle, walking through this journey

The illusions, the believe
The miracles why we seek
Wake up to reality
What really matters you shall see

Life, has no meaning
What matters only the breath we take
Life happens despite what we create
The problems and troubles, all self-made

Don't judge, we all make mistakes
We complicate life with desires we make
For simply it stands for the peace of mind
Understand this and you lived your life

Like the river flows to make oceans
Life goes, on and on till the end comes

3 am

~ Precious ~

3am, past midnight
Here I am
Fully awake, fully aware
In the verge of silence
Soothing yet frightening
The darkness became so alive now
With thoughts and imaginations
The recall of all memories
The remains of the past
There is no one with me at the time
Yet, I don't feel alone
I feel many emotions
I feel, I am alive today
The sound of crickets
Frogs and trees
As if they are calling me
As if I am one with nature
I am in the place I want to be
One with the universe
Time hasn't stop
While I stare to the dark
The room becomes colder
I become wiser
While I lay to the floor at peace
Its 3am past midnight
Here I am
Fully awake, fully aware

Became a Creator

~ Precious ~

So lost on the thoughts
Burst illusions on a rush
Like gust of wind cross
Crushes the mind with the fuss
With belief you're not enough
Clogs the instinct you once trust

As the memories flow
Time froze, became so slow
Show's vision that you know
Chose words that will blow
Forwards rhymes as you throw
Grows to sentences in a row

The clock's ticking
Tricking the brain into sleeping
Erasing words after nitpicking
Pushing the limits into thinking
Seeking imaginations to sync in

An escaper, with pen and paper
Adding some labor, a poetry maker
Because of traitors, so many haters
Became so greater, light as the feather,
Flew up and became a creator

My child

~ Precious ~

My child
Oh my child
Your so young for this world
So young to analyze the selfish
The dark side not been told

My child
Your gonna be strong
But for this you have to face
Difficulties of life ahead
Go through things now unsaid

My child
Your gonna get hurt
Trust broken and people lost
Realize pain is not only cuts
But also when the heart suffers

Through loneliness and thoughts
Life becomes hard, some days are dark
But child life is short
You will rise and make it worth
You'll be different and be kind
Shine your light through this world

My child
Oh my child
For now your so young
To analyze what life is
Sleep for now, Sweet dreams

Let it go

~ Precious ~

Let it go
The rage inside of your heart
Caged like a roaring lion
Craving the destruction
Creating hatred

Let it go
The envy towards other
The jealousy, the agitations
Clinging onto attachments
Sources of greed and desire

Let it go
The controlling towards life
Being anxious or depressed
The despair inside the heart
Emptiness of life
Negative thoughts in mind

Live freely, we are all the same
Let it go my darling
Let it go

Deep

Deep is a poet from Bangalore, India who rediscovered his love of poetry after many years when he joined our group: Become a Published Poet in 100 Days. He is an animal lover and a vegan. Deep hopes his poem will inspire other to reflect deeply about treating animals with respect and dignity.

Don't participate!

One by one removed from their station,
Their hearts beat boom, boom, boom,
Like a massive violent explosion.
Heading wretchedly towards their doom,
They amble along in desolation and gloom.

They die a million deaths watching their sons
and daughters,
marched to slaughter.

They die a million deaths as they hear blood-
curdling screams,
and watch blood flow like dirty water,

Let's feel their intolerable excruciating pain,

As blades slice through their flesh and vein,
bodies torn apart and hung upside down
to let all the blood drain.

There are no monsters or demons,
Just us humans.
We choose their fate,
When we participate,
And put their flesh on our plate.

\- Deep

Mir Atif

Mir Atif, comes from Kashmir and living here comes with a grassroot experience of surviving in the epicenter of various layers and deep-rooted conflict in the subcontinent. Started writing at 13, today has over 100+ poems, short stories and abstract pieces. Mir has been a founding member of social work club that has been helping the society since 5 years now. Mir since college has been volunteering many international organizations. If fortune ever knocked the door for Mir ever, he would work on the food problems faced by people on this planet, and he dreams of a day where no human sleeps hungry, of a day when there will be no famine hit countries.

Stripped

Your gaze left a mark on my soul
Your smile is a scar across the face of my heart
A mark on my body is your being
Like an un-calligraphic tattoo beneath my skin
Your prying glance-Strips me down
Peeling – slowly, shredding
the last walls of dignity
shabby corner - in the motel rooms
of my mind, near the mirror
where we brushed together &
visited the darkest corners
I look for signs
of you, for your memory to come
and ravage me, for my pain
glows in the dark
but would you ever know?
Now I stand naked, there.
My soul nothing but ash
On a secluded place, is the bridge of grief
Over the waters of heartache
A perfect place for lovers to go
they jump to death
in the moon lit night
by whose shadows
you once undressed me
marvelled at the falling men and women
amid shower of dead stars
I stand in lonliness
Arrant, naked, threadbare, Nothing to show
But the insolvency of my love, upright madness and
longing for your pain just so that your memory
can ravage me

Notes from an unfinished love!

To unlove and love you
Took me to hell and back
Weak need not to attempt
No tests for desires to know
All that remains
Is but a distant dream
Like that of a story
That was rubbed off
The only remnants
are pencil marks
At the bottom of that plain
paper
That once carried
uncaring written notes
Of an unfinished love
It reads and I write it now
'love her' till the gentle rain
Falls in time to her
soundless tears
'love her more' when winds
wreak havoc
And ferocious is the thunder
She is as the note says
A pendulum that swings
Between fear and
suffocation
Sometimes fear and
abandonment
At times faith and infidelity
'love her' when she watches
clocks
Chases time
'love her more' when she
tries
Tries to make the broken
pieces fit
Tries to make sense of it all
Amid the notes lives a
memory
Of her fighting demons
Slaying those dragons
And yet at times
She like a child
Terrified alone in a big
world
'love her' for her bravery
'love her more' when she's
scared
Like the chronicles of a
Death foretold and of
Endless battles to find
herself
The note that hints
of her when she is small
and of times she feels
huge and invincible
'love her' when she feels
too much
'love her more' when she
feels not enough
The unfinished love that
Speak volumes of ache
Pain and anguish,
Of her eyes that grow dim
And when she is a bright
light
Letting wind weave magic
Through her hair
Inscribed in that note's heart
Were two, sometimes three
Words
Love her, lover her more
'love her' when she's light

'love her more' when in
darkness
'love her' when she loves
you
'love her more' when she
hurts
'love her' when its easy
'love her more' when its not
The pencil with its broken
nib
Wrote for me to understand
Understand her, it spelled
She offered you her fragile
heart
She didn't need you

She had chosen you
The note now breaths its last
Asks me to love
'love her' when she doesn't
love
'love her' for she is her
'love her more' for you
know
How to love harder
Undying wish of the
Love that died
Keep the notes
Of the unfinished love,

Grief's Note

Through withered gardens I
went
Climbed the highest hills
saw snow peaks in crimson
colours
Jackboots drenched in blood

The valley that once was
was bare than deserts now
As if in the darkest hour
It saw the face of death

swayed to a secluded place
Caged in the unfinished
rooms
Grief's note was written in
bold
On the unending wall of
pain

Taken back to the exact
moment
Where everything
succumbed to regret
When veins were snapped
And nothing could be saved

Forsaken even by loneliness
today
I recall that teeming city
Who took its fervour
Who drew the first blood

Ashes tell the story
Ruins bare witness
Who lit the fire first
Who hit the last nail

Attacked by arrows
That spew venom
The half drawn daggers
Still tripling with blood

The fate was sealed
of smiles and her children
their dying kashimir
was sent to dungeons

home died in the arms of the
visionless summer
the year of the blind that
hollows you out
I feel in my chest, my heart
may squeeze
Yet from hell's heart I stab
the oppressor

Unrest 2016, Kashmir.
From the notebook of grief
22/9/2016 : 22:18 hrs

Famine

As the hope dies
Inside the eyes, of hungry stomach
The child who waits to perish
You got nothing but anguish
Crying that child, and me
Will these tears help?
Will the sufferings flee?
Tired of sympathies
Your tears & distresses
Will you not act
You don't even react
I die, I am dying
When I see the planes flying
With my muted voice
Amid my soundless cry's
I hear the bangs I smell the soot
I look at you, amid jackboots
Write injustice, you be the sly
My blood will Inscribe revolution
Over the skies.

Nameless from Yamen

My Pen

It starts to cease
Blinking of an eye
Back on the plains
In the land of pure
Under the golden dome
I'm thinking back
I wanted to scribe
But my ink just froze
Under the blood moon and
sky
When the moment's stop
I cannot fly
Imaginations were torn
Where are you
My Imam
I ask
Your separation
I cry
Is denting me,
And my shouts
have hallowed me
And my muted cries
Call your name
Give me wings
Take me back
Under the golden dome
In Karbala
Beneath the blood moon
and sky
I want to feel
Your presence
I yelp and long
For your holy scent
And nearness I yearn
Again, and that touch
And that kiss
On the zareeh
That blessed zareeh
And thank the man
Who is and will
Be legend for some
Greatness for others
For me, my Imam
My reason for life
For justice who stood
Who gave his life
His kith and kin
Had morals so high
Had love so much
Epitome of mercy
I send my salutes
For the one who saved
The saviour they say
Of the divine message.
I am coming back
To you my imam
Your love be the ink
My heart the nib
And I shall write
And continue to write
Written
during my visited to the
Largest peaceful gathering
in the world
Arbaeen, in Karbala, Iraq

Hajj Qasem

In the Year of Zainab
You gifted your soul to Hussain
And left us aseer
Like the children of Hussain
You lived like Qasem
You left like Qasem
Goblet of death was Honey
You preached like Qasem
Sea and the people were same
Like it was Ashura
Waves like emotions claim
Kullo Yomin Ashura

Your life a lesson
You lived like Ali
Your death a lesson
You died like Hussain
Ah! How Sakina would've felt
Seeing the Alam go down
Defenseless, shredding even
The last ray of hope
We don't feel any different
Seeing you go away

During the matrydom of Hajj Qasem

'My Poet

The grizzly eyed
The rare prophetess, drew me
The shape of my heart
Made love to me
The way she wrote poems
Rhythmic, sensual & imaginative
Each stroke of her pen
A gateway to my nirvana
Her absence around me
Reminds me
Of her presence inside me

Zephyr

Sitting across the table
With a faceless memory of you
Like a diffusing musk
From the bower of your lips
Conclusion of eternity
Caged and uncaged
Zephyr made home
In the corner of my heart
Only to give rise to
A horde of frenzy
Your memories like chains
Taking me to gallows
To which I willfully submit
As the home is
Where the heart is

What fun is to die a Painless Death!

Laila, signed a treaty with fate.
Headsman was proud
The injury fatal
Your sentence
fate whispered unhurriedly
'complete separation
Of head from body'
Capital punishment
For loving me
The scene was set
They walked you
To the executioners block
From far away
I looked and found
Solitude in you
His lips started to move
My last wish
'let the sword be blunt
And the executioner clumsy'
silence
and the air was filled
with the smell of death
-Laila

She cried to sleep
I came consoling her
In her dream that night
She moved her lips
Those beautiful lips
Why the sword so blunt?
And executioner clumsy?

I looked at her
My stare comforted her
I wanted multiple strokes
While they severed my head
I wanted a prolonged death
A more painful one
For what fun is to die
For you - if it were painless.
-Majnun

Did Anything Change?

Smiles of the heaven
Have the children of conflict.
Eyes full of dreams
Had the children of conflict?

Bliss of severance
On that eventful eid
Silenced by a death foretold
Remembrance makes the heart
to bleed.

Like waves of frozen Dal
Rainin' tears to bid farewell
He was brought to rest
Where the undying dwell

Day 50 today
Feels like day one
He clings to stones
You can hold that gun

He came in the hue
of the holy shroud
And the flower of passion
Made Kashmir proud

At lidder they vow by the
waters edge
Standing side by side they took
this pledge
The land of saints now breeds
new heroes

A lane without name today is a
sedge
Listen to his name
With all your heart
And hear that song
Which your ears did not

Day 50 today
Feels like day one
Do all that you want
You're back to square one

Grief is in a hurry
And pain passes by
Vanity too busy
Left to bewail n cry

In the valley of death
Where flowers don't mourn
They took his dreams
with pellets they torn

That child can't see, he sure
can't scribe
You've blinded him and he
asks instead
In a knife-like tone he hoists
his voice
Is he not big enough? To honor
his dead.

Day 50 today
Feels like day one
Did anything change?
Excuse that pun

Natassha Halil

Natassha is an aspiring poet from Malaysia. Growing up, she has an affinity to English and has been interested in the language ever since. So, although she's Malay by race, her native language is English. A certified crazy cat lady, Natassha's definition of a perfect day is getting lost in a good book with her fat cat next to her. When she's not reading, she'll be writing instead. Seems like she has a thing with words. There's only one way to describe her. Immersive. And that's what she hopes to illustrate in her poems.

Truce (25.10.2018)

What is that I hear you say?
It looks like things begin to flutter away
Smiles and laughter can be misconstrued
With sorrows kept far from the truth

Pick it up. Gather yourself
No time to rest. No way to lose your breath
Whilst you're wandering into pensive
That's when it slips through your fingers, you won't believe

I yearn for forevermore
I'm looking for miracles beyond the moor
With an old tree standing ghastly in the field
Where have all the leaves and flowers been?

Let's get ourselves out of trouble
Our awkward steps shouldn't tremble
This heartache will be tucked deep inside
Until finally all of it subside

It's OK to be afraid
The smoke will eventually make its way up the chimney
Once all the confusion decay
There I will find me

Unprecedented (25.10.2018)

Smitten
That's exactly how it feels
As if bitten
By a cat appearing from nowhere
You can only find true love in fairytales
Or more like beneath a dragon's tail
That's how mythical it is, nobody knows whether it's real
Maybe it's somewhere out there
Waiting in the dark crevices, waiting to strike
At the time when you're most unaware
But it's a pleasant surprise
You can't figure out what it is until you start to try
How long can this feeling last?
Nothing in this world is ever cast
Hope can be your enemy or your friend
But what prevails is faith in the end
You have to be patient
If you want to see it unfold
Something so suspicious, so massive truth be told
Be warned you may end up dead
Then again who cares we said
The idiosyncrasy is for us to find
And we will interlock, keeping it bind

Doubt (25.10.2018)

All covered from head to toe
This is the moment when you bow your head and let your heart know
The inkling of a conversation in your heart
It's with God right from the start
But then you see your presence here
As if scrutinised by strangers and peers
You start questioning yourself whether you're thinking too much
Or are there eyes out there ready to judge
How ever can we find solace?
When even in His holy house there are bollocks
That sinking feeling wondering whether people are sincere
Or am I here just to adhere?
I'm just another weakling. Whose full of doubt and strange things
As much as they look at me, but aren't I doing the same to them?
Deep in my heart I think I know
There's something so much bigger He wants to show
It's not about me, it's not about them
It's whether you would want to comprehend
The connection is actually between you and Him
In the moment when you're lost to fault the world then
We don't realise that we are blinded
By things we don't know and yet kept quiet
So take a step back and then you'll see
The place we live in is not as bad as it seems
Be joyous with the wonders that He's given
Count your blessings so you will be driven
To tread the path which you should
Even at times when nobody would

Reborn (09.11.2018)

Look out the window
On a fast moving train
What do you see?
Do you watch the terrain?
Or is it your reflection that you see?
Dragging your feet off the ground
You take one step at a time
The demons inside are beginning to crawl
Wanting to let out what's confined

Frantic looks to the left and to the right
The feeling of anxiety is starting to come by
But you can't control the undying excitement
Of the treachery you're going to do tonight
You're about to sweat, slowly loosening your tie
This is not right
Yet you gulped with greed, wanting what you might

Knock knock. The door opens
The fruity scent of champagne escalating your
yearns
Your deepest desire stands in front of you
With scintillating perfume that bursts your brains
You slowly begin to sink
In pleasures you never knew exists
Heart's beating fast, breathing's becoming hard
You know this is all deceit
But you can't bring yourself to come to part

No need to be scared. Set your heart free
You're in a safe place now
As long as there's no one here to see
Move fluidly, speak amicably
How quaint...
A sinner is born into this world

Ancient Kingdom (18.11.2018)

Melancholic skies and shady haze
Faint drops of innocent dew, that was when I walked into an ancient city
As if lost in time, I was awed and amazed
Of the beauty of a hidden place lost in history

I slowly paced myself admiring the buildings
Walking on arbitrary paths
In the midst of it my mind kept wondering
What were the secrets kept from the past?

Each minute passed by, all I could see were pretty things
From intricate handicraft to scrumptious foods
I got lost in thoughts, wants and longings
My eyes were sinfully sensed I didn't know what to do

A river existed so calmly at the beginning
It spanned to bigger ones as you get in deeper and deeper
Wooden boats arched with rooftops, aged yet stunning
Either parked or rowed lazily, and so many of them they divide and conquer

As I walked further down, gentle cries of children's laughter filled the air
Lovers huddled together capturing their romantic moments
I witnessed these lovely scenes adorned by the amazing trees, where their leaves are turning into red affairs
How I wish I could stay here and remain dormant

The villagers were indeed a creative bunch
From native workmanship to exquisite embroideries and tapestries that told stories
Let's not forget the delicacies full of flavour and crunch
Eventually everybody needs to fuel their tummies

An ancient city is not complete without its temples
They stand majestically, strong against the test of time
People come and go, praying for their hopes, dreams and desires
I show them my respects
With an invisible red thread, wishing for what I longed for to intertwine

But the time has come, the bell has rung
It was time to set sail, leaving to a different destination
Hesitation was overbearing as my heart sunk
Given the chance I want to stay here forever, elated with passion
I can never find a place so beautiful and serene
With its cold breeze caressing my skin

So many nooks and crannies left unexplored
I knew this was a sign for me to come back to this place which I've learnt to adore
Maybe next time it will be with those whom mean so much to me
Until then, 'tis a bittersweet goodbye oh ancient city

Chrysalis (11.12.2018)

We are born from a chrysalis
Curled up, pure and white
Not knowing anything, not knowing what is might
Slowly we grow only from milk from a tit
In the strong arms of a mother who carries us oh so dearly
A man roams near and far
To look for sustenance for his wife and children
All the blood, sweat and tears made worthy
Whenever he comes home to his family

A life is taught of the ways of the world
How to stand, how to fall, how to rise above it all
Little by little, it permeates
Into something we believe in, something we create

And then comes a time when reality happens
There are so many differences, some more incomprehensible than others
We venture out into the unknown
Even when mother and father said no
Over there we discover many things
Things that are complete opposites to what we believe in
Experimentation of desires and sins
The risk of not knowing what it brings

We finally meet a crossroad
An inescapable choice we have to make
What will this become of me? Is this certain as my fate?
When all hell breaks loose and you're at that moment of despair
That's when you meet someone who really cares
You share the same words and breathe the same air
That's when things become clearly beautiful
A bittersweet affair
A strong resolve upon treacherous roads
Together we both rode
Towards a future filled with uncertainties
And yet a future that we want to believe

A relationship is conceived between a man and a woman
And as done by our forefathers, this life is repeated again
But now with children which we call our own

Preach (06.11.2019)

You say your piece
You think it's right
But you bark than you speak
Do you think that's might?
Sometimes it's good to stop and listen
It's not really about being even
But you want to win, like a shopping spree
When the real virtue is to agree to disagree

You think your voice matters
But they don't
Like a toddler fighting over an ice cream cone
Look at yourself in the mirror, tell me what you see
There's nothing. Just debris

Contrition (06.11.2019)

Run, run. Run away…
There's something you're fearful of. Needless to say
Keep it precious. Like a diamond in your breast pocket
Better yet, keep it secret in a locket
You're afraid to go to the atelier
Just in case it'll be valued. And you're thinking gruyere
Me, me, me. It's only for me
I don't care what everybody sees
Rough on the edges, finally it cuts you
But why? Am I not special to you?
Twiddling thumbs, you think it's for you to have
When in actual fact, it isn't yours to bear
You should just let go. Or let it be
But no. You're consumed with greed
One day it disappeared and you find it no more
Heartbroken. Shattered to its core
Instinctively, time just passes by
And there you are. No chance to say goodbye

Raj Nishanth

Raj Nishanth is a poet who is from Tamil Nadu, India. He considers his faith and family to be most important to him. Growing up, he was fascinated with music and this interest led to some early exposure to reading/writing. Later, due to some tough experiences of life, he developed passion for writing and started writing poems which reflects different colors of life. Other than this, he is passionate about cooking, playing keyboard and photography. And now, he is beginning his journey of writing here humbly with a strong belief that his creation will touch his reader's soul. He believes that Love and gratitude alone can lift one's life to greater heights!!

Pleasure of Imagination

Let you close your eyes
Dream the stars in the skies

Spread yer feathers together
Flutter, flutter, and fly to ether

Smile all the while & be flattered
That keeps you always glittered

Lively dolls and toys are your company
Get what yer want more to accompany

Get on the flowers made dhow
There the stars are waiting to tow

Listen to what spirits bow
Strives to keep you at wow

Jump down on the winged gee-gee
It's for you to free-thee!

Just get caught into the maze
There you have much to amaze

Ginormous clouds are your dais
It's your turn to roll the dice

Dozy vices are always nosy
You "The Ballsy Queen' are always
rosy

Wear the snazzy precious crown
It's only for u to enthrone

Keep your soft sole on the Velvet
nappa
And drink yer sweet, delicious cuppa

You're at the peak of the cusp
It makes all others gasp

You've waxing crescent for piggyback
And tailed comet to leapfrog

This is what we call a wonderland
Decorate this splendorous dreamland
With your giggle studded garland

What you adorn with here
Are all imponderable pleasure
It's the Culmination of real human
treasure

The Swing

Sitting on the swing
I swing I swing

No one is here with me
To keep the swing to swing

The sole hope is the rope
Which I've been tied to

Sitting on the swing
I swing I swing

As I'm tied to the tree of dream
My ambitious eyes amply gleam

Hanging above the wild stream
I'm looking for the swing to extreme

Sitting on the swing
I swing I swing

Gusting winds slaps my face
Fisting splashes slows down my pace

Clueless vision threatens my mission
Seamless thought allows an egression

Sitting on the swing
I swing I swing

Now, it's not fair climbing up
It means to me more than winding up

The endless sky is up there
I'll never despair & fly around the sphere

A call with no words

It's a calm morning
Silence hasn't broken
Me with her on waves
She says just hush!!
No words between us
Beats bump the ribs
Sole breath rushes
Whole world stuns
Unseen emotions
Unheard quietness
Eyes see nothing
Senses are lost
Thoughts overboard
Minds on telepathy
Presence felt
Beyond belt
Numbness has ruled
Silence continues
Calmness prevails
Sailing souls
Crossed oceans
Fuming passion
Attains mission
Love is speechless!

Coffee

Can't start my day
Without kissing you
Can't move ahead
Without smelling you
Sugary bitter blends
Seductive, inspiring,
Aromatic fragrance
Such a dark fantasy
Every drop of you
Soaks through filter
Mingles with cream
Add shades to foam
Holding you tightly
Leans on you gently
Taste you slowly
Every sip of you
Slips through my lips
Wakes up my taste buds
Refreshes all my nerves
Enriches my shady soul
Let my day rock & roll

Dramatic Proposal

This is from the crazy fellow
To the heart-stealing mellow
Giving you a handful of mallow
Under the green shadow of willow
I am not an unworldly callow
That's not letting you follow
If you wish, I can be your pillow
If you push, I should be a hallow
Come and green my grey fallow
Blow your love and fill my hollow
My love for you is not shallow.
Allow your heart to sink-slow

Moon Loves Sun

You are my sole source
Wish to touch you in the course

I can't shine without your light
You're the spine to ever lit

Though I revolve around the earth
I'm in your orbit and be in the mirth

Reaching you is my incredible goal
Your every beam touches my soul

Who kept me very far from you
It always keeps me feeling blue

Many are there to love me
I always wish you grabbing me

Yes, the moon loves the sun
Yet, you can't stop the run

Romantic Solace

My longings miss me
when you're with me

My sorrows go away
when I see you sway

My heart smiles
when yours trails

I love to glance
When your eyes dance

My indeed love reins
As the romances rains
It's not all about gains
But real drain of pains

My hesitation expires
As your comfort inspires
No need for any despairs
As the love in us respires

Feared of your flimsy gazes
As they often leave me in mazes
The love in your sparkling eyes
Paints my heart with delightful dyes

Melancholy

I feel so hot and chill
I have no smile to spill
Thrills don't stay still
Pain enthrills my gill

I have a vacuum to fill
Yet, that's not my will
Let that ever be nil
I don't bear anymore kill

I was under a spell
Fascinated me to dwell
It's where the joys swell
Wishing that'd ever swill

Life should flow as a rill
Humbly with no-frill
I free myself from thill
I will do what I will

Love

The fragrance of love
It's meant to plow
To plant the seed
& let the joy breed

It flows and grows
As all raise the brows
It blows and glows
As it slowly mellows

It is so sweet
Nothing else can beat
The steps of all feat
Resounds in our heartbeat

There're no bounds
That's how it sounds
It spins you around
It'll ever be the found

It keeps you happy
It shows you snappy
It drives you peppy
Not wrong to be sappy

Fall in love
Sink in love
Sing in love
Live in love

Agony

Something sometimes
Have gone beyond
What I guessed
Nothing has happened
Anytime as I wished
Searching for the way
For the sheer bliss
I often lose myself
In the rush

Gently,
With neat collar and cuff
I'm a regular victim of bluff
How long
Can everything be puffed?
It's nice to snuff
Instead of being in a huff

Frequently,
I float in the dream
Smoothly,
Like a boat in the stream
Although
I'm good at the helm
At last,
I run out of steam

Indeed I'm not aimless
But rhythm-less
Damn it! Who said I'm useless?
Nevertheless, I'm gain-less

Why should I hear
Other's words
I want to live
The life of the birds

LDR

I'm not alone anymore
I tell you what furthermore

She is a pretty gritty donkey
Made me a sassy crazy monkey

She speaks with emojis & gifs
Her punches are my precious gifts

We fight for nothing
Argue for everything

Always, there lies something
Which implies a true thing

Not knowing each other well
Not sure how happened the fall

She likes my usual nature
I like her friendly stature

We are going back to our ages
Filling in some missed pages

Approaches are at a snail's pace
Togetherness wins the race

She is the reason for my bliss
Yet, I'm missing a true kiss

Every thought of mine carries her
Every moment of me be with her

Wish this love last forever
And brings us all pleasure

A Desperate Child

I'm not your child
So you behave to me wild

I'm not your blood
So I won't deserve any good

I'm not from your womb
So you curse me to the tomb

Though you are so unkind
I feel your pain and mind

I neither wanted to have cared
Nor be the reason for the hatred

I can bear any kind of pain
I have gone through all strain

My emotions have become numb
I have no words and be dumb

I have no tears left to shed
I admit I'm a living dead

I wonder why humans have 6th sense
I could find more love with the 5th sense

Mother to me is a utopian angel
She will never be my real

All I need is a simple life
But mine hanging above a bloody knife

Foodie

I wonder why
I have a single mouth
I'm a super spy
Reveal any food underneath

I'm a simple guy
Giving up all dietary oath
I eat a lot
& regret aftermath

I'm not
Good at math
That's why I don't count
How many times I eat
It's easy to clean my plate
As nothing will be left on it

Food is an expression
Calms down your depression
Encourages sharing
Energizes all with caring

Please don't be in hunger
& let your tummy, a terrible singer
Never let anyone in hunger
Share even if you have a burger

Food is my love
Taste is my passion
I die for delicacies
& I crave sweets
Love being a foodie
That makes me a goodie

Rehna Mathews

Rehna is a poet from Canada. As part of her journey to her true self, she rediscovered her love for poetry. Through writing, Rehna was able to get in touch with her intuition and creativity. Rehna believes that poetry and creative expression are the key to unlocking love in the world. Rehna has an amazing daughter and beautiful cat who inspire her every day to be herself.

Let's Fly Away

The airplane glides in the air
As I sit in trepidation.

A pandemonium of thoughts in my head.
Should I have stayed?
What is this nervousness?

I glance at the clouds floating carefree.
A sharp contrast to the heaviness in my being.

As I stare at the beauty of the sky
A voice whispers
Close your eyes
Take a deep breath
Surrender and go with the flow.

This is who you are.
The spirit of adventure awaits you
Wanting to feed your soul
To feel like a child again
Eyes and heart filled with the wonder of the unknown.

Excitement fills my heart
As my true spirit rises up.
I am not afraid anymore.
The world has opened up to me
And I am ready to fly.

To My Daughter

When I first laid eyes on you
Oh how I fell in love.
We were miles apart
But I was determined to see you.
That day finally came
When I finally met you.

The fear in your eyes.
The love in my heart
Wanting to take you away
To comfort you.
To make you mine
No matter what.

You are my soul
Transcending time and space.
I want to hold you for ever
And never let you go.

Your laughter, your joy
Your tears, Your love
You are my reason to live.
My heart is crushed
Every time you leave me.

But my child, please know this.
Our stubbornness may drive us apart.
But my love will never leave you.

A Beautiful Painting

When you first saw me
You knew you had to have me.

I saw the look in your eyes
As you admired me.

Next thing I know.
I was coming home with you.

I remember you beaming with pride
As you hung me on a wall.

For days after that
You would stand proudly
Looking at me and smiling.

But as more time passed
You saw me less and less
As life came in the way.

The dust has settled
But I am still here watching you
Wondering if you have forgotten me.

I am sad right now
But I do know the time will come
When you will walk up to me
And we can be a family again.

Eternal Love

Love is who we are.
Love is what we do.

Our beauty in eternal
In every form of life.

Like stars in the sky
The colors of the rainbow
The flowers in the meadow.

But what happens to love
When we compare?
What happens to love
When we discriminate?

In all our beauty
How can one life be better than another?

Where is love
When we put down another life?

Let's transcend and see each other for who we truly are.
In a world that is pure
In a world that is imperfect
Where there are sounds of laughter, drums and dancing.
Let's bring back our world of love

The Cycle of Life

I am a leaf on a tree
Born in a branch.

The sun rays of my youth
Gives me a vibrant hue.

I dance in the breeze.
I watch the world pass me by.

Sometimes I get hurt
Sometimes I get blown in the wind.

I still stay strong.
Till autumn when I change again.

This time I am different
But still the same.

The day will finally come
When I will leave the tree.

This is the cycle of life.
I will be gone
But a new leaf will be born.

A Walk to Reflect

The orange rays of the sun
Touches her skin.
The birds chirp all around her
Entertaining her with their music.

She walks in silence
Her feet feeling the sand
Her gaze staring downward
Too many thoughts in her mind
Too many things to accomplish.

She crosses her arms
And starts walking faster
A sudden sound startles her.
She turns around
A little child smiles at her.

You are beautiful, miss
She says and skips away.
She stares at the child for a while.
What a beautiful moment!

She looks up at the sky.
This time is sacred
Everything else can wait.
She uncrosses her arms
And looks to the warmth of the sun.
She continues walking
This time with a smile.

Goodbye Old Friend

You came when I needed you.

You held out your hand
As I lay on the floor dejected.

I was lost in my own darkness
With no sign of light.
You lit a candle of hope
Enough for me to see again.

You've held my hand
As I fought to get up.
You've been my shoulder
To rest my weary head.

You believed in me
When I didn't see my worth.
You wiped away my tears
And smiled as you did so.

I can never forget
How you saved me.
Gratitude fills me
As I think of you.

Even though we walk separate paths
You are always in my heart.
Every time I feel down
Your memories will always carry me through.

Ode to Writing

My work is done
I now relax.
I take a deep breath
This is my time.

What should I write about?
The answer is inside of me.
Pen and paper in hand.
I start to write.

The words flow out.
Wait, are those my emotions?

I need to hold back.
What will they say?

Keep writing, don't stop.
Let it flow.
My heart feels light.

I look around
I hear the birds outside
I see my cat
I hear my daughter.

Could this be anymore perfect?
My words are now on paper.
This is my moment
This is my poem.

Divine Feminine Energy

You are a Queen
Full of life
Full of love.
You are a Goddess
Full of grace
Full of majesty.

We look at you in wonder.
The sun shines upon you
To show you off to the world.

The stars oh how they sparkle in your eyes
Your words give us comfort
Your tears cleanse our soul.

You are powerful
You are truth
Bless us with your strength
Speak life into all of us.

Let the world say what they want
Let the world try to put you down.

But you, magnificent Queen
Fix your crown
And keep shining.

Tribute to Poets

The world is vast
Yet I was surrounded by loneliness.
I knew I was different
Maybe that's why I did not belong.

I yearned for love
I yearned for acceptance
Rejection after rejection
I slowly built a wall
And stayed in silence with my soul.

And then you came to me
A star in my dark night
Reaching out your hand.

I feel the intensity of your love
Burning through my walls
Melting away my fears
Making me alive again.

The world is just you and me.
Our hopes and dreams
Out there for us to experience.

I don't know what the future holds
But I am certain of this
Your heart is where I belong.

Swekchha Luitel

Every time her mother brought her a new notebook, the first page would be the hardest one to write for her. Once she breaks the ice, she feels more confident with each subsequent page. Moving to a new country offered her a fresh start, but it did not come easily to her. Moving to New York, from a country like Nepal (both in terms of culture and geography) the journey was parallel to writing in her notebook. However, she has been surviving well on her adventure so far. Currently, she is residing and pursuing her Bachelor's degree in Queens. Forever humble and kind to others, she is grateful for having found this wonderful global family of poets away from her home. And she loves her mom a lot!

In the curves of life, look how strong I have become.

In the curves of life...
Look how strong I have become.
There are many folds.
Some of them were upfold,
and some of them downfold.
But it amazes me how my courage works.
Challenges are even wondering
with the guts of my resilience.
Tortures, punishments, and outcasts
none of this cruelty could break me.
Even the shadow of mine
screams at the utmost attempt
to win life's both best and worst tempt
that is to bring me down.
But no matter what the struggles
I always manage to stand up straight,
and shine with some giggles.
And the giggle so genuine
that even misfortunes would leave me alone.

| Swekछा |

Butterfly.

There is this sudden pain when I see you tonight...
Probably this pain they would call the butterfly.
Then when I picture these butterflies,
I see them flying inside my belly.
But as they fly...

Why are their wings making cut in my muscle tissue inside?

| Swekछा |

Change.

Something inside me
went through a stormy blizzard,
when I hear, you want to change.
Maybe I am afraid that you might change.
Change... what we have
Change what we might have.
Most of all, change us.
Please change if you need to.
But change with me.
Allow me to change as well.
I am ready as you are next to me.

Come on, let's change together
But never change being apart.

| Swekछा |

This extraordinary love.

Had I never laid eyes on him,
I would have never fallen in love with him.
I would not have fallen for that difficult, painful
Heart aching, extraordinary love.
And don't ask me to fall out of that love.
If I could, I would.
I would a long time ago, if only I could.

| Swekछा |

Silence.

There is silence that you love, there is silence that you hate
There is silence that relaxes you, there is silence that suffocates you.

And then with all these shades of silences
there is a miracle that you will never have
And yet there is a miracle that you will always have.
Looking at a child so new... to this world,
who is not even a day long.
They are so smart enough to understand motherhood.

Mom, I knew you

from the very first second— I landed on this earth.
Mom, I knew you — from the very first time I cried.
Mom, I knew you — from the very first smell I smelled.
Mom, I knew you — from the very first sight I saw.

A lotta times, mom,
I am being called a miracle,
but Mom, you are a miracle to me.
Yes, you are a miracle to me, Mom.

| Swekछा |

Mom, this is for you!

This air is all a lonely air for me...
If it does not have your smell in it.
I can never feel home again,
Until and unless I inhale the same air you exhale...

| Swekछा |

This one is for you.

You came to my world with some grins,
color yellow, and happiness all along.
Then you carried some butterflies,
a ten million fireflies, and one moon.
For those you named it for me all along.
You hold me cozy and warm,
wrapping me inside your arm.
Like a caterpillar wrapped inside the cocoon.
You treat me so well like a gentleman.
That all my feathers were healed
And so, you are this refined man.
You let me fly,
Just as beautifully as butterfly.

| Swekछा |

This one is for you, too.

You were someone,
Someone who would eat snow with me.
Someone who I can trust with my stone.
Someone who I can call my carrot!
Some who has stuffed me with love so much,
That I started looking like a stuffed toy— all soft and loved.
And you were my ranger all along— tough and protective.
But I have lost you like I have lost my dreams without you.

| Swekछा |

Erotic Sound in my Head

Finally meeting you the other day
underneath the sunset and some shadows of these trees,
I looked through your eyes,
and all I see is those soon to be fading memories of our time.
For you, I learned that I did not matter as much
But I thought of this much
that we could be together, may be for a little longer.
But seems as though you no longer ponder
upon the bittersweet memories of our time.
I was embraced, but I was only embraced superficially by you
I mattered, but I only mattered superficially to you.
I see you liked running your fingers into mine.
And I was wanted but I was only wanted superficially from you.

All this came across to me -- so vividly
When you poured upon her so undoubtedly
that is when I concluded. You and I,
we landed, but we only landed superficially upon each other.
Our bodies were there one after another
on top of each other,
but never did our soul could assemble us
in such a way that you wanted me.
But you wanted me never fearlessly.
In fact, you once told me that you did not want me for a reason,
and the reason was for the fear of losing me... forever.
How could you want me so much, yet never wanted me enough?
that you could not win upon your fear of losing me
How could you want me so much, yet never wanted me enough?
that you could not collect confidence in not losing me... ever.

| Swekछा |

Why wait for a hero? Let's become one!

Why do we only in expense of a hero,
bring change in this world?
Why does it always take a life of a hero,
to maintain humanity in this world?
Why does it always take the struggle of a hero,
to bring positive vibes to this world?
Why do we only wait for the appearance of a hero
to bring revolution in the world?
Why can't we ourselves, think of being a hero
and initiate spreading kindness in the world?
Why can we not take inspiration from a life of a hero
to make possible difference in the world?
Why wait for a hero? Let's become one!
I am sure there is a way out of it...
And more than that—
I am sure we could do better!

| Swekछा |

Oh, Dear Nature Mother!

Oh, dear Nature lord,
Would you make it rain tomorrow?
I want to sleep deep with its drippings.
Would you make it snow next day?
I want to play sledge on the frozen mountains.
Would you make it fall after that day?
I want to cuddle on the dry leaves of these trees.
Would you make it green occasionally?
I want to forget all my pain staring at those.

| Swekछा |

You're a mess worth having...,

I am no longer a child,
No longer a naive,
No longer an innocent,
And, no longer adorable.
I am an adult

With many of to-do-lists to take care of
But even more than that bills to pay off...
I try playing hide-and-seek
like for the old times sake
But it ain't fun anymore
They look for me no more...
I used to run to my mom
If I get hurt,
But now I run but I run
To hide it from her
Wish I could erase all my to-do-lists
Wish I could erase all my wannabes...
Wish I could be a little selfish,
Where I could wish to have happy endings.
And there is where it would end
When I hear someone saying
Darling, you're a mess worth having...

| Swekछा |

some bitter-sweet Memories,

The key is to release it — But what if you really cannot?

There are going to be several trials and errors. However, trust the soul inside of you, and be patient with it. Let it take time. Also, keep reminding your soul that the purpose is to let go, eventually.

| Swekछा |

I hope this Tramway of Love reaches to you!

Like Love, he arrived like a cotton candy sky
And then in my dream like a moon in the midnight.
Like Love, he came clam
And been and stayed clam this whole time
Like Love, he never touched me
And yet understood me just like my mom
Like Love, it was all easy
And never felt like as if we even tried
Like Love, even his departure does not change a thing for me
Because I am still here thinking he is the love of my life
Like Love, we are growing
Even though we are apart, we are growing together.
Like Love, we are meant to a forever
May be not in a reality, but we are in memories alive forever

...

When you were with me —
You never made me miss my dad or made me wish on how much
he was otherwise.
When you were with me —
You healed all my mishaps, and childhood scars.
When you were with me —
You just not loved for my physical appearances,
but also, and mainly for the broken child inside me.
Thank you for loving me truly...
At least now, I get to say — I have been loved once
And I have been loved truly.

...

From straight lines to curves. Through thick and thins.
From plains to up and down waves.
Throughout you are seen from darkness to the brightness
And you will be seen anyways and, in all ways,

...

| Swekछा |

Dear Reader, got some a quick question!

What's Age?

It is just the number, but experiences you come across could be indescribable sometimes.
What's it for you? ______________________________

What's love?

It is deep, yet pragmatic. It comes in all shape and size. Sometimes it is outnumbered, and other times it is deserted out with none.
What's it for you? ______________________________

What's life?

It is an adventure that is mined as you grow with it. It is iridescent.
What's it for you? ______________________________

What's family?

It is not just about blood but instead a bond. Like for intense, one of a kind that I found from my global poetry family, here. It is roofed with love, comfort, and inspiration.

What's it for you? ______________________________ |

Thank you for answering!

| Swekछा |

Twila Richards

Twila is a writer from Canada. She is eclectic in her style of writing and strives for uniqueness. She loves her children (Marin and Misha), family, dogs (Angel and Foxy), and friends, which are her inspiration. Twila has written two plays, short stories, children's stories, and too many essays. She loves teaching each and every one of her students. Advocating for learning disabilities is a passion of hers. She loves this family of poets.

Up Mix

by poet who has dyslexia (Twila)

I have tone deaf blindness;
in radioactive silence
feeling my way around in the light;
allowing the things that are a fight
the putrescence in the air settles to the ground,
as I walk it around
There are times that I let my thoughts wander,
to free be to ponder
today is one of those days of embracing my
doom,
as the light is turned on in the dark room.

Haikus

Per•fect•ly thought out
syl•lab•if•ic•a•tion makes/
cre•ates great hai•kus.

Zig•zags zig•zag•gers
zeal•ous•ly
zig•zag•ging
zeds
zon zoo•keep•ers' Zen.

So, I am surprised,

as you are not here with me,

by my fleeting joy.

By: Twila

Tommy (Prince)

Dear Tommy,
  I wipe your tears away.

Tommy, dear Tommy, you were taken,
                                   you were stolen,
                                   you were forced from
                                   your home.
                                   You were taken,
                                   you were taken to Elkhorn RS
                        where you slept
                        where you slept by Dummy Bad Boy,
                                   you slept by all the buried
                                                               children,
                                   your "heathens."
                                   You slept, were
                                                               kept,
  a few feet away from your relations.
The children who lay dead; not ever   forgotten.

Tommy Dear, how did you survive?

Tommy, dear Tommy, you survived,
                                   you survived to wander,
                     to wander your way; however,
                                   you were always turned
away.

Tommy, dear Tommy, you volunteered,
                                   you volunteered to serve,
                        to serve your country.
                                   You volunteered for those
who had no care?

Tommy, dear Tommy, you scout,
you brave,
you fought for the
Devil's Brigade.
No need to polish; you felt shards 600 feet away.

Tommy, dear Tommy, you laid the line.
you laid the line,
to hold your fist up high.
Three days,
three days,
three days the score!

Tommy, dear Tommy, you went in deep.
You scout, great shots!
Great shots,
you great company!

Tommy, dear Tommy, you're tired,
so tired,
yet you got on with might.

Three days,
three days,
three days once more
to fight, to capture 1000 Nazis in corps.

Tommy, dear Tommy, your medal
your star,
fleeting honours; hurt to the core.

Yet Tommy, dear Tommy, you fought once more.

You brave,
you fought once more.
Tommy Dear, how did you survive?

Tommy, dear Tommy, you returned
to your land to train.
You trained
just to survive
once more
Tommy, dear Tommy, the hero,
who you are,
you saved, you saved
before your fall.
You fell,
you fell
you fell with the drink.
You were lost,
you were lost
'til you survived no more.

Tommy, the Prince, which is who you are,
I say your name.
I call your name
to honour,
to give honour, to honour you I must.
I wander, I wander 'til you are found.
Your bust, so
solemn, stands still right on your land.
In honour, in honour I call your name as
I wipe your tears away.
Sincerely, Twila

you love me cuz I love you

You left it out for me.

You left it out.

burp

So, I ate it,

it was good,

delicious.

What's that…?

RABBIT, RABBIT!!!

lick

There was a rabbit.

Do you make more for me?

I still 'ungry.

What?

That was yours?

lick

That's okay

cuz you love me, cuz I love you.

Is there more?

By: Twila

Crazy Canuck

What can I do you for?

Yep, I'll tell ya a stereotypical story of me, a Canadian. We are folks who like taking the four-wheeler mud-bogging. Some of us enjoy rippin' it up all over hell's half-acre. In a hot second, many will want to hang and we'll pick up our buds in one of our four by fours to go to Timmy's to order a double-double (mine is always a single triple). We sure love our Timmy's. That's for sure, for sure.

So, I am now from the Peg. I used to be from the Gap, but I like it here 'cept for the winters. There's a reason why they call it Winterpeg. When you wear a beanie here on a minus 45 days, you'll then start respectfully calling it a toque.

The snowbirds won't return 'til the spring with their Florida tans. I can't seem to blame them, especially with the dump we got last night. Speaking of which, it's still dumping, which is good 'cus I'm about to go tobogganing with my canoe before I go ice-fishing.

In the summer, we go for a Slurpee and a beavertail. It costs more than and loonie and a toonie, but it is worth every cent. Sometimes I'll grab me some pop and a box or two of Smarties. Dang those are good.

Summer is the session of road construction as the potholes are a doozie and dang it, when I drive over one, I get all kerfuffled. I especially do when my bud decided to go giver over one with his stick-shift goin' 120 klicks. 'Fr*ckin' eh, Bud?' is what I asked him 'cause my head hit the roof. That was my last time takin' a rip with him.

His brother is such a hoser, too. He likes to make puppies by screwing the pooch most days. He is sometimes racked on the chesterfield all day watching 'Schitt's Creek' and only getting up to go to the bathroom. Once I caught him cuddling up with a stuffie! Good grief! He tried accusing me of having a favourite stuffie and I told him 'Yeah no!' Well, he's kinda embarrassing specially when he wears rubber boots instead of runners.

Once we went for a two-four or two six, but ended up getting a micky of Goose and a bottle of Crown. He had to use the liquor store's washroom. Dangnabit, he has to go a lot. On the way back he was going twenty klicks over and got pulled over by the Mounties. I was riding shotgun and wishing I wasn't. The Mounty was in a good mood and let him off Scot-free. Un-fr*ckin'-believable.

That night, I got lost in the sauce while we were watching the game. The Whiteout is happening and the Jets won the game. Unfortunately, I woke up with a splittin' headache. The only sure fix was a Timmy's with my single, triple. It is the fix for sure, for sure specially before we got to go skidooing.

Well, that pretty well wraps up my story. I hope I honoured Canadians in some way. For those who have difficulty understanding it, sorry.

(For: Kirsty, Suzy, and Leanne.)

Contronyms

She was puzzled by the :Puzzled
puzzle that she was
puzzling over until she
puzzled it out.
<She was confused by the game that we was problem solving over until she figured it out.>

Weather: I weather the
weather, which
weathers my home.
<I withstand the conditions, which wears down my home.>

Fine: Fine dining is only
fine to kids. <Great food is only okay to kids.>

Overlook: The manager seems to overlook
the needs of those he is to overlook.
<The manager seems to ignore the needs of those he is to oversee.>

Dust: Please dust
the dust after you
dust the cupcakes.
<Please remove the dirt after you apply powder to the cupcakes.>

Table: I table that we
table the
tables.
<I propose that we revoke the idea concerning the tables.>

Transparent: It is transparent that the
transparent clock is useless.
<It is obvious that the translucent clock is useless.>

Watch for Rime

As I search for you my brother,
(There is no one to bother).
The stagnant air has a slight wind.
I rummage for clues with none to find.
My heart aches for your love,
when I see the bodies don't move.
This place looks like an open tomb!
On I fumble and on I comb
the places marked with flies.
How can I forgive my enemies?
The stench makes me cough
and gag even though
I smile. As now
I know.
I have hope to give
that you are alive.

Painting with Letters

by: Twila

po-et-ry (pō'ĕt-rē) *n.* **1.** that form of literary art which expresses lofty thought, feeling, or action in beautiful language; **2.** composition in verse as opposed to composition in prose; **3.** what poets create; **4.** art with letters.

Peplynn the Penguin

To: Misha, Marin, and Vincent　　　　From: Mom/Twila

Peplynn the penguin who wanted to fly.
"I know I can do this, I just wanted to try."
But the more Peplynn tried,
the louder the others cried:
"Everyone knows that it looks like fun…"
"BUT, it simply cannot be done."
Peplynn did hear this,
So, the penguins did miss.
For off he did sneak,
to the highest peak,
where he did climb,
and climb,
and climb.
From there he flew...
down, down to the ocean blue.
In the freezing cold,
he became extremely bold,
as he did cry,
"I will FLY!"
He did not stop,
as he waddled to the top.
This time he ran
(with an impressive wingspan)
and then… he flew
down, down to the ocean blue.
In the freezing cold,
There he did scold,
"I need something new,
I just don't know what to do!"

With feet before feet,
he felt his mission was almost complete,
as Peplynn did climb again
to ponder what to do.
Something wonderful happened just then.
For at the top
(where he did stop)
Peplynn did slip,
and went off a lip.
He then flew!
Down, down to the ocean blue.
Just after the splash,
he did have to dash.
For a sea lion was looking for a meal.
This Peplynn would deny,
as he could fly!!!
in the cold ocean blue.
Then all the penguins knew
(when the sea lion stopped by)
that Peplynn, the penguin, could fly!

Meander

I ere, a
' ing h th n Twila
m w k e r e, d e me.
a l v Follow
er where.
Y

Vincent Choo

Vincent is an inspirational writer from Malaysia. He is an out and proud member of the LGBTQ+ community and owning his HIV+ status. He empowers and uplifts his community with his bubbly and charismatic character. Strutting through life with his head held high and sprinkles glitter of joy to the people around him. He actively works with local NGOs to raise awareness on HIV preventions and provides supports to people living with HIV. He loves lolling on a beach, a comfy chair, a good book in hand, a cup of coffee on the side, a groovy jazz album on stereo and a good laugh. Drawing inspiration from his life, he pours his heart in writing as a form of journaling and healing, in hopes of spreading love all around.

North South East West

When in doubt,
The north star guides my sail
When in turmoil,
The south lake froze to tranquility
When in pain,
The east wind breathes in life
When in despair,
The west end sings to a new dawn

North South East West
These are the counsels in effect

10 Steps to Coming Out

Honest finally
Embrace gracefully
Confident immaculately
Strut sadistically
Dress fabulously
March proudly
Dance freely
Safe eventually
Love ultimately
Here to stay, ABSOLUTELY

More less

More Joy, less tears
More Grace, less curse
More Compassion, less judgment

Love More, fear less

Love is Love

Who doesn't love Love
I love Love
Everybody loves Love
Love is Love

The Boy Next Door

[If only I had offered him Chai]

When he walked by, my eyes will pry
Dreamy eyes and sweet as pie
When he said hi and offered me chai
I was shy and pinched my thigh

It was July when he said goodbye
Moved from Shanghai to Dubai
There I stood high and dry
Loss of words nullify

Out of sight and out of mind
As years gone by in Mumbai
We met again eye to eye
There we were just you and I

In my mind, he offers me Chai
But there we were just passerby

Blank

Pen tapping
Keyboard clacking
Time ticking
Mind scrambling
Eyes straining
In the end. Nothing.

Rumours

Whisper that rings
Word that stings
Travel with wings
Wreckage it brings

Jason, Tyson or Edison

The heat of passion
Sounded like Jason
But he was bespoken
What a waste of flirtation

The heat of passion
Sounded like Tyson
He was a republican
Clearly there's no salvation

The heat of passion
Sounded like Edison
The perfect gentleman
He became my poison

Be it Jason, Tyson or Edison
They're all in my kitchen
Maybe we could have a foursome
Opps.. Wouldn't that be awesome

Blackouts

Madness tiptoe
On frosty snow
Seeds it sow
Lunacy grows

One says go
One says no
Two tangoed
Like battle calls

Sharp falsetto
Shaky vibrato
Muffled pizzicato
Confusing concerto

Rational defense fold
Impulse takes hold
Like ducks in a row
Leading to my woe

Fists I throw
At my mighty foe
Like dominoes
Trickle I fall

Losing control
Bitter swallow
Agony echoes
Darkness befalls

Penguin
-Vincent & Mir

Walking in a line
In the snowy beads
The gentle birds
Marching to the beat

In the grizzly eyes
Bubbly they seem
At the end the world
Playing hide and seek

The Story of a Goldfish

Once there was a goldfish
Who felt outlandish
Wanted to fulfill a wish
Then it perished

A Cat's Purr-pose of Life

I've got the paw-er
I've got the purr-sonality
I've got the cat-titude
Live long and paw-sprer

Serenity

Journey Begin
Healing Within
Peace Therein
Quiet Herein

Sandcastle

I live in a sandcastle
Built with grains of hope
Structured with imagination
Mighty and grandiose

Then came the wave
Swooshing my castle away
Though it never seems to stay
A new castle is underway

Rainy Day

Dedicated to Twila and her lovely students

Drip drop drip drop drip drip drop
Lily's little head pop and bop
Drip drip drop drop drip drip drop
When will this rain ever stop

Rekindled

Notification popped
Decency exchanged
Past reminisced
Conversation flowed
Curiosity peaked
Plans made
Where does this lead, I thought?
Only God will know

The Boy Who Wore Pink

It was early spring
The boy wearing pink
Sitting on a swing
Tears on his chin

Poison he drinks
Hollow as he sings
Flying without wings
Condemn was his sin

As his world spins
He drowns in gin
Patience wearing thin
All he needed was a
win

Broken violin
Blood in his ink
Riot on the brink
Like balloon on pins

The harder he thinks
The further he sinks
Sanity he clings
Where was his King

As his spirit shrinks
His eyes wouldn't blink
All he wanted was to
scream
But he was dead
within

Only if it's just a dream
Like a movie on screen
Somber was the
theme
Theatric in extreme

Rope on the beam
His legs dangling
Nothing in between
It was obscene

He was seventeen
His name was Jean
The boy who wore pink
His light went dimmed

Say a Little Prayer

Through troubling waters
One foot after the other
Hope be your anchor
Courage is your cover

Soaring higher
Venturing deeper
Nurture your color
In search of answer

Do me a favor
Never surrender
Take no prisoner
Storm the weather

Eyes on the future
Pasture be broader
Together we're stronger
In truth and honor

Perfectly Imperfect

I am perfect when
I accept that
I am imperfect

Countdown Poem

Wind Down

5 things to be grateful today

4 treasured happy memories

3 reasons to say I love you

2 friends who shoo the grey

away

1 new adventure awaits

Vincent

Acknowledgements

Thank you to Amee Bee for the customized logo for our room 'Beautiful People and Words'. A special thanks to Twila Richards who selflessly took on the task of putting this book together. Also, thank you to our children: Marin, Misha, and Yuvika. Thank you to our family and friends who supported us in this journey and encouraged us to reach for the stars.

And last but not the least, thank you to my family of poets who contributed to this book. Be proud and enjoy this moment. We did it!!!

Rehna

www.ingramcontent.com/pod-product-compliance
Lightning Source LLC
LaVergne TN
LVHW051010080826
845145LV00009B/2543

* 9 7 8 1 7 3 7 7 4 6 0 0 3 *